# I Learn to Obey Rules

Carolyn Nystrom

Illustrated by
Dwight Walles

MOODY PRESS
CHICAGO

© 1990 by
CAROLYN NYSTROM

All rights reserved. No part of this book may be reproduced in any form without permission in writing from the publisher, except in the case of brief quotation embodied in critical articles or reviews.

Moody Press, a ministry of the Moody Bible Institute, is designed for education, evangelization, and edification. If we may assist you in knowing more about Christ and the Christian life, please write us without obligation: Moody Press, c/o MLM, Chicago, Illinois 60610

ISBN: O-8024-6172-7

*Printed in the United States of America*

1 2 3 4 5 6 7 8 Printing/DP/Year 94 93 92 91 90

"Rules, rules, rules! I'm sick of rules."

I could hear my older sister storming in her bedroom, slamming drawers, doors, and words around the room. Lisa was having a bad day.

I walked to her open doorway and waited. Her dark hair stood straight up with anger.

"What do you want, Timmy?" she snapped. But I could see her eyes soften. I know that Lisa likes me—even when she's mad at everything else.

"What went wrong?" I asked.

"It's dumb rules everywhere I go," Lisa exploded. "At school, I just wanted to go to the library to work on my report. School rules say I need a hall pass, but I lost it. So I got sent to the principal. He made me stay after school. Mom's rules say that I have to call her if I'm going to be late, but I didn't have money for the phone. I knew she'd be upset with me. So as soon as they let me out, I biked home as fast as I could. But on the way, I got stopped by a policeman. He lectured me about traffic rules and red lights."

I had to agree that Lisa had had a hard day.

"I've had it with rules," she stormed. "Why can't we all just do what we think is right?"

I liked Lisa's question. It started me thinking about rules. I wondered: Are rules good or bad? Why do we have rules? Who started the idea of rules? What if one rule says the opposite of another rule? Are some rules more important than others? Is it ever right to disobey a rule? Should we try to change rules that we don't like? Will we still have to obey rules when we are grown up?

Lisa and I talked about rules a lot over the next few days. We talked with Mom and Dad too. We even talked with our pastor. Here is some of what we found out.

*Exodus 32:15-19; Deuteronomy 10:3-5; Exodus 20:1-17*

Rules started with God. Long ago, God told a man named Moses to lead thousands of people on a long trip across a desert. They were going to a new land that God would give them. God knew that the people needed rules so that they could live together without hurting each other. He knew that they also needed rules so that they would know how to please Him.

So God called Moses to a high mountain. While Moses was there, the whole mountain shook. There was fire and smoke. Then God talked to Moses and explained the rules He wanted His people to obey. God wrote ten commandments on two tablets of stone. Moses carried these tablets down the mountain and gave them to his people.

*Proverbs 1:8*

It is hard to like rules. But as Lisa and I talked, we had to agree that many rules, even the ones we didn't like, were good.

Lisa said that if no one needed a hall pass at school, lots of her friends wouldn't go to class at all. And if Mom didn't ask her to call home about being late, dinner would not be ready when she got there.

I don't like Dad's rule that I have to spend half of every Saturday helping him with house and yard work. But I've learned lots of jobs on Saturdays that I'll need to know when I'm grown up and have my own place to live. And I like being with my dad.

*Proverbs 22:6; Ephesians 6:1-4; Proverbs 23:22*

All families have rules. God put people in families so that they could love and take care of each other. He gave parents an important job. Parents must teach their children what is good and right. And they must teach so well that when the child is grown up, he will still do the good things that his parents taught. And parents should try not to make their children angry.

Children have an important job too. They must try to learn from their parents. They must respect their parents and not make the job of being a parent harder. And children must obey their parents—as long as the family rules are not against God's rules.

*Proverbs 20:11; Proverbs 15:20*

    I don't always like my family rules. My friend Steve can ride his bike as far as Front Street, but I have to stay in my own block. Some of my friends can play outdoors in summer until nine o'clock. But I have to come in at eight thirty. And none of my friends has to work on Saturday.

    But I do like some of my family rules. Mom lets my friends come inside my house to play, and she even gives them snacks. Steve's mom only lets his friends play in the yard.

Each family has different rules. Children have to get along with their own parents. But it's all right to tell your parents if you'd like them to change a rule. Most parents will listen to why you feel that way.

*Romans 13:1-7 ; 1 Peter 2:13-17 ; 1 Timothy 1:1-3 ; Titus 3:1-2*

Schools and towns and states and countries all have rules too. Rules help make places safe for the people to live. God wants His people to obey those rules and not cause any trouble. My school rules make the school a safe place for me. I wouldn't want to go to a school where people could hit and kick and scream whenever they wanted. I might get hurt. School rules are one of God's ways of taking care of me.

Schools and towns and states and countries all have someone in charge of them. That person might be a principal, a mayor, a governor, a president or prime minister, or even a king or queen. God allows these people to have their jobs. He calls them His servants. Even if we sometimes don't like what these leaders do, God wants us to pray for them.

*Matthew 22:15-22; Acts 5:12-32*

But not all rules are good. Once, long ago, Peter and some other apostles were standing outside the Jewish Temple in Jerusalem. They were teaching everyone they saw about Jesus. They were even making sick people well. Many people there believed in Jesus.

But the leader of the Temple was angry. He made a rule that said, "You must not teach about Jesus." And he put Peter and his friends in jail.

That night God sent an angel to Peter. The angel said, "Go stand in the Temple again. Keep telling the people there the whole story of Jesus." Then God opened the doors of the jail and let Peter and his friends out.

The next morning Peter and his friends were back at the Temple talking about Jesus. They said, "We must obey God rather than men."

*1 Corinthians 7:21-24; Ephesians 6:5-9*

God wants us to change bad rules if we can. Long ago, many people who became Christians were slaves. Rich people owned them. The slaves had to do any work their owner said. The owner could even sell them or kill them. The apostle Paul told these slaves, "Get free if you can. But if you can't, then be a good worker for your owner. Remember that God is Master to both you and the person who owns you."

Some Christians today live in countries where laws do not allow them to buy a Bible, or to go to church, or to pray aloud, or to talk about Jesus. But God's laws say that His people must study the Bible, and worship with each other, and pray, and tell others about Him. Christians in those countries have to choose whether to obey their government or to obey God. We should pray for these people, that God will keep them safe.

*Romans 3:19-20; Romans 5:19-21*

God's laws help me to know when I've done wrong. Last week at the store I saw a bright pink pencil with different colors of lead. I started to put the pencil into my pocket. But God's law says that I must not steal. So I took the pencil back to the shelf. Maybe if I save my money I can buy it later.

Yesterday, my mom asked, "Timmy, did you clean your guinea pig's cage?"

Cleaning Hippo's cage is a smelly, messy job, and I didn't want to do it. So I said, "Sure, Mom, I did it yesterday."

But God's law says that we must tell the truth. So later I told Mom about my lie. Then I cleaned Hippo's cage. At least I have a happy guinea pig.

Obeying God's law is hard sometimes. It was hard for Jesus too. But Jesus always did what God wanted.

*Deuteronomy 5:29; Isaiah 33:22*

    Some of those rules are God's special laws for His own people. God said that He must be their only God and that they must treat His name with respect.
    But other rules that God gave to Moses show up as laws all over the world. Many countries have laws that say,

"You must not steal, you must not kill, and you must not tell lies about someone." Even people who do not know God use those rules. They know that these rules help people live and work together.

God told Moses that if His people obeyed the laws He gave them, life would go well for them—and even for their children.

*Hebrews 13:16; James 4:17; John 13:34-35*

Obeying God's laws helps keep us out of trouble. But keeping out of trouble is not all that God expects from His people. God also wants us to do good. When my friend Steve was sick with chicken pox he had to stay home from school a whole week. He couldn't be with anyone who might get the disease. Steve got tired of staying at home. He didn't want to play with his own toys. He got bored with television. And when he got bored, his pox itched even more.

I've already had chicken pox. So I packed a box full of my small cars and trucks, and I stacked up my puzzles, and I took them all to Steve's house. Then we played together. Steve's mom was glad I came to visit. I think Jesus was glad too.

God's rules tell us what not to do. But they also tell us what we should do. God wants us to do kind things for each other. He wants us to love each other.

*Matthew 5:17-18; Psalm 19:7-14; Psalm 119; Philippians 3:20*

God's laws never change. Jesus said that as long as there is heaven and earth, God's law will stay the same. The laws of countries and cities and schools and churches and families all change. And that is good. A law made by people can have mistakes. So the people change the laws and make them better.

But God's laws were perfect from the beginning. God gave them to us because He loves us. God's laws show us the right way to live. They show us how to love each other. They show us how to praise Him. They help us to get ready for heaven.

One writer in the Bible prayed to God, "Oh how I love your law! I think about it all day long."

I don't think about rules all the time. But I'm glad God gave them to us.